LIFE IN BRAMPTON WITH
LIZZIE
THE WITCH

LIFE IN BRAMPTON WITH
LIZZIE
THE WITCH

DAVID MOORAT

HiP
HISTORY INTO PRINT

First published by
History Into Print, Unit 19, Enfield Ind. Estate,
Redditch, Worcestershire B97 6BY in 2019
www.history-into-print.com

© David Moorat 2019

All rights reserved.

ISBN: 978-1-85858-353-2

The moral right of the author has been asserted.

A Cataloguing in Publication Record
for this title is available from the British Library.

Typeset in Haarlemmer MT Std.
Printed in Great Britain by
Cambrian Printers.

CONTENTS

	Acknowledgements	6
1.	Introduction	7
2.	Some facts surrounding Lizzie The Witch	10
3.	Local stories attributed to Lizzie The Witch	25
4.	Witchcraft: A dark art?	40
5.	... Or a confidence trick?	41
6.	So, true or false?	50
7.	Witchcraft over the centuries	51
8.	Conclusions	67
	Bibliographical references	68

ACKNOWLEDGEMENTS

I am greatly indebted to many people who have been so helpful during the course of research for this publication: Staff at Cumbria Archive Office for their patience, forbearance and professionalism; Stephen White of The Lanes Library, Carlisle, giving access to The Jackson Collection and many other sources of information; to the many folk of Brampton, and to my personal friends who have urged me on and given much support when my spirits were low.

I am much impressed with the work of Stephen Warnes, BA; RGA – our local artist, who, having carefully read the text, has created the very impressive covers both front and back. I am also very grateful to Jean Warnes for her diligent proof reading and advice on presentation.

Following on from the successes of *Life in Brampton with 63 Public Houses* and *Life in Brampton with the Dandy*, many people have been urging me on to complete *Life in Brampton with Lizzie the Witch*. It is both an honour and privilege to record such aspects of our local history which form part of our rich heritage.

Work now begins on *Life in Brampton – the Battle of Hell Beck*.

David Moorat

Chapter 1

INTRODUCTION

Bent with age and with the assistance of a stout stick, a crooked old lady, dressed in black, is making her way slowly down Craw Hall into the Market Place of Brampton. She is wearing a red cloak with a hood that is trimmed with white fur. People are moving out of the way to let her past – avoiding any opportunity to annoy her. She is on her way to meet two young girls who are eager to know who it will be that they will marry. This ... is Lizzie the Brampton Witch.

Craw Hall, Brampton

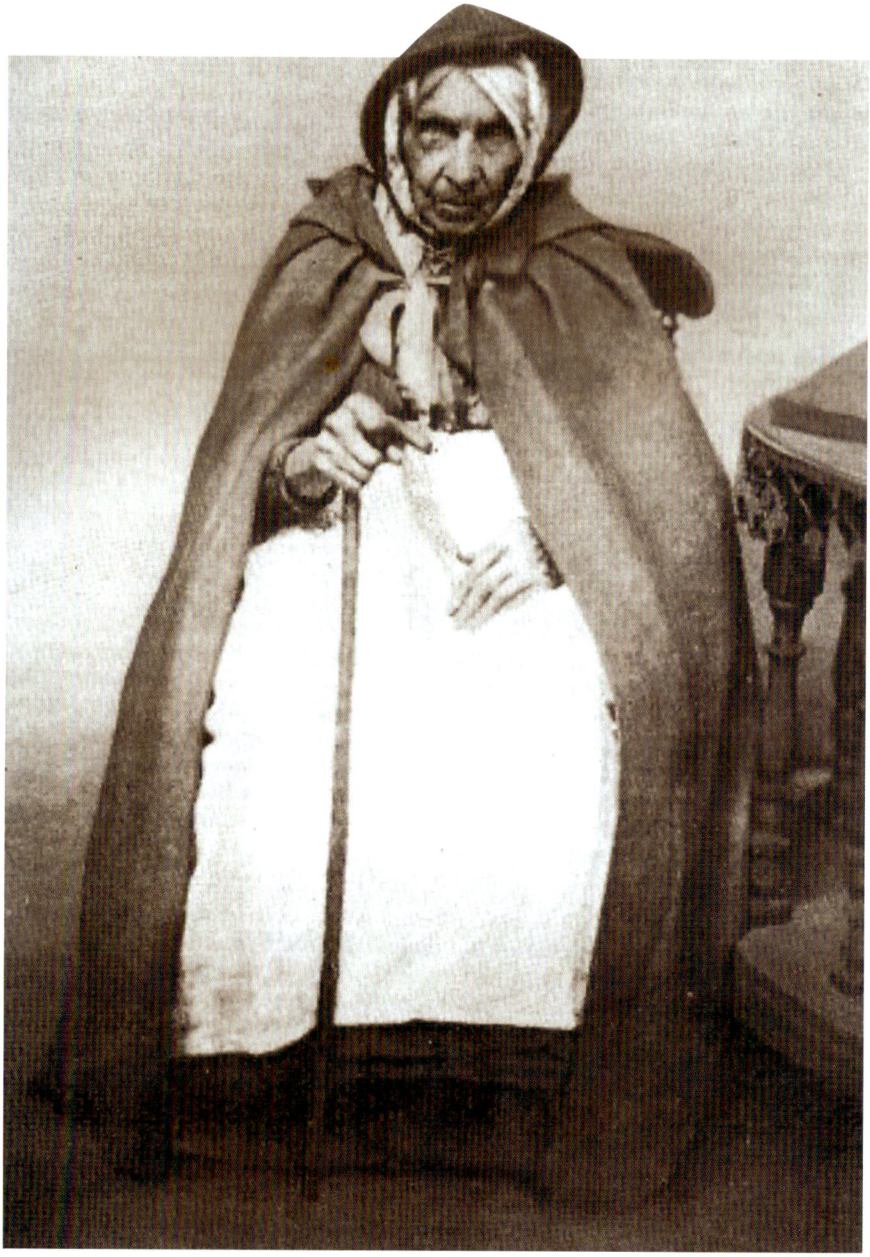

1. INTRODUCTION

Many stories exist about Lizzie, but what can we really believe as fact, and what might be pure invention?

Lizzie Baty was one of the "wise women" or Sybils of Cumberland, who obtained great notoriety in her day. Various articles have been written about Lizzie – this book serves to collect these together; to attempt to establish what is fact, what might be fiction; and to encourage an open mind. Numerous tales and authenticated anecdotes have been handed down over the past 250 years relating to her "second sight"; witchcraft, or whatever people may wish to call the strange power that "Old Lizzie" appeared to possess. In so far as some of the anecdotes are concerned, the limits of an open mind may set the boundary, beyond which some stories become pure invention, perhaps embellished over time. However they are part of our local heritage and deserve preservation.

Chapter 2

SOME FACTS SURROUNDING LIZZIE THE WITCH

We can start with some indisputable facts which are confirmed from primary sources e.g. archives:

Birth records exist, recording that Elizabeth Douglas was born in 1729 at Castle Douglas.

Peter Burn, a distinguished Brampton Parish Councillor, church warden, draper and poet, gave lectures on various aspects of Brampton life in the 1830s, and recalls a personal discussion he had had with a Mrs Tinling, Lizzie's neighbour at Craw Hall, who had enjoyed a close relationship with Lizzie Baty for many years.

Lizzie had told Mrs Tinling about her earlier life, having been born and brought up in Castle Douglas. At the age of twenty she had eloped with John Baty, a local schoolmaster who was 8 years her senior. One dark winter's night when snow covered the ground, she made her escape out of her bedroom window by means of sheets that she had tied to her bedposts. After leaving her home that night John and Lizzie passed through a churchyard, where suddenly Lizzie's courage began to forsake her and she was overcome with anxiety. Lizzie described to Mrs Tinling how she had knelt upon a grave to say some prayers before continuing their journey, eventually arriving at Kirkbeckstown near Bewcastle in October 1750.

2. SOME FACTS SURROUNDING LIZZIE THE WITCH

a) But, some questions immediately spring to mind ...

First – Why should John and Lizzie go to so much trouble to elope and rush off from Scotland into England to marry? At that time, in Scotland, consenting couples could marry from the age of 16 years with or without parental approval. Since both were over 20 years of age, choosing to elope might suggest that either Elizabeth's or John's family were most likely to have disapproved of their association and were about to make efforts to prevent the marriage from taking place. Meanwhile, across the Border in England, marriage required a couple to be resident in a parish for a certain period of time, during which Banns of the proposed union would be published in church on three occasions prior to the ceremony – giving the opportunity to anyone to state reasons for objecting to the marriage.

Second – After having eloped together and having arrived in the Bewcastle area, why did they choose to live in separate houses? There is significant doubt as to whether the two actually lived together immediately, as on the 25th November 1751 records of Stapleton Church show that John Baty was living at Kirkbeckstown, whilst Elizabeth's address was given as Nixonstown.

```
Nov 25  Baty, John, Kirkbeckston  p Bew-Castle, school-master.
        Douglas, Eliz, Nixon's Town    do                        [Stapleton
        Hoodless, James, Brampton, in-keeper.
        Afft dated 24th, bond 25th.
```

Diocese of Carlisle – Marriage Licence / Bonds 1740 – 1752
Cumbria Archive Service

These two small groups of houses were approximately a mile apart. Perhaps this was a deliberate attempt to avoid any person objecting to the marriage on the grounds of immorality – the couple co-habiting together prior to their marriage.

LIFE IN BRAMPTON WITH LIZZIE THE WITCH

Nixonstown

Kirkbeckstown

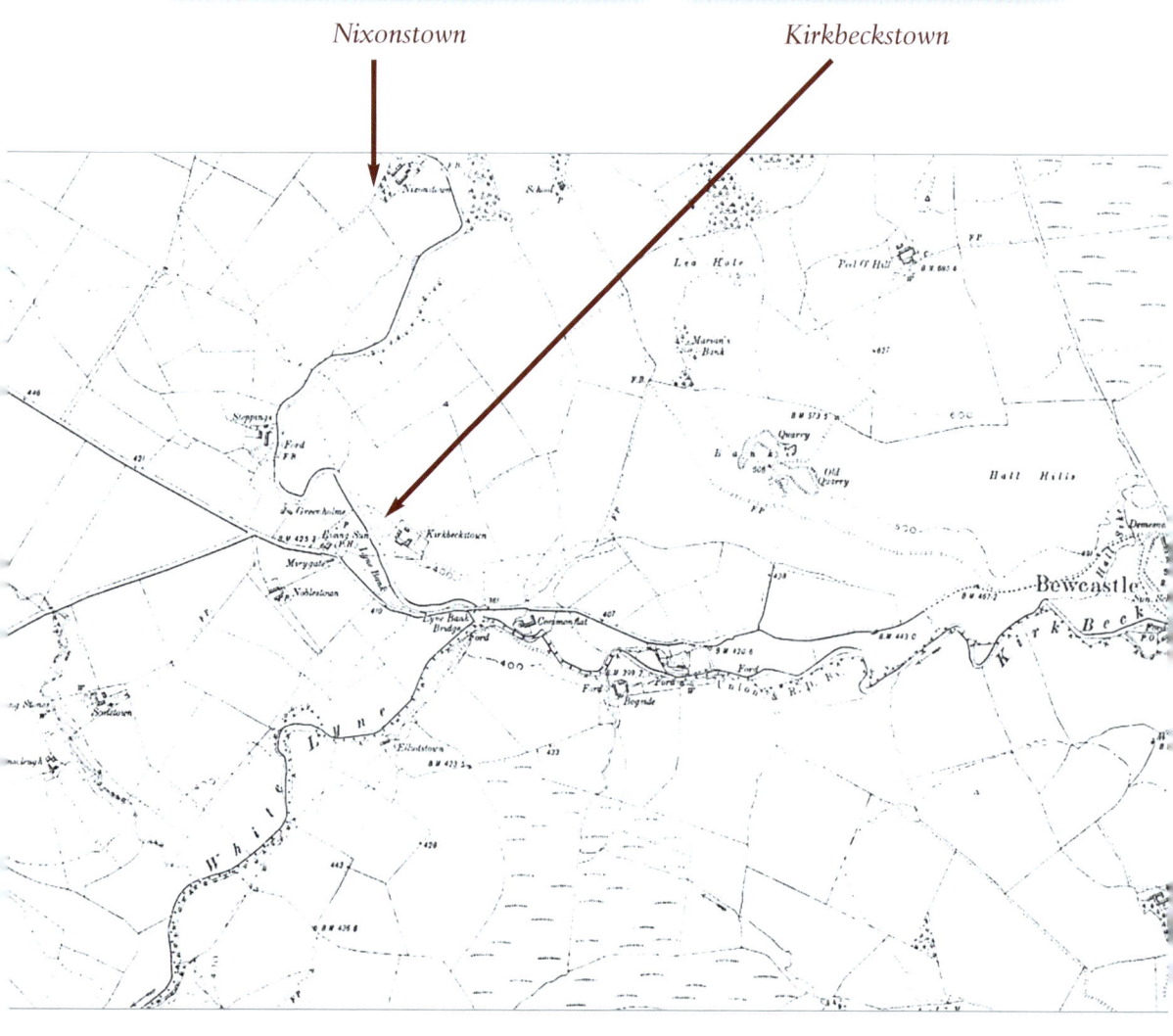

2. SOME FACTS SURROUNDING LIZZIE THE WITCH

Third – Why, after having crossed the border into England, did John then arrange for the marriage ceremony to take place **immediately** without following the usual course of having banns read out in church three weeks before the wedding?

A special licence called a "Marriage Bond" was applied for, by John in Carlisle on 25th November 1751 at the cost of two hundred pounds (an enormous sum of money at that time) so that the marriage could take place without the need for banns to be read out for three weeks. Conditions of the bond required that neither of the applicants was to have a criminal record; that both willingly agreed to the proposed union; and that a "bondsman" would be required to confirm the legitimacy of their application, and that they accepted all legal and financial consequences in the event of their application being found fraudulent. James Hoodless, a Brampton innkeeper, is recorded as the bondsman and an affidavit was signed by all three parties, with the marriage scheduled to take place in Stapleton Church.

> *"Know all Men by these presents that we* **John Baty of Bewcastle parish, schoolmaster,** *and* **James Hoodless of Brampton, innkeeper** *are held and firmly bound unto the Right Reverend father in God* **Richard Oshaliton** *by divine permission Lord Bishop of Carlisle in the sum of Two hundred pounds of good and lawful Money of Great Britain to be paid unto the said lord Bishop dated this twenty fifth day of November in the reign of our Sovereign lord George the Second, by the grace of God, of Great Britain, France and Ireland, King defender of the faith and so forth. The condition of the above written obligation is such that if there shall not hereafter appear any lawful let or impediment, by reason of any pre contract, consanguinity, affinity or any other just cause whatsoever, the above* **John Baty** *and* **Elizabeth Douglas, both of the parish of Bewcastle** *in the County of Cumberland may lawfully marry together. And, that there is no suit depending before any judge Ecclesiastical or Civil, for, or concerning any such pre contract. And that current parents or other governors of the said parties be thereunto obtain. And that they cause their said marriage to be openly solemnized in the* **Parish church of Scaleby between the hours of eight and twelve o'clock in**

the forenoon. *And do and shall save harmless and keep indemnified the above Lord Bishop, for and concerning the promises: then this said Obligation to be void and non effect or else to be and remain in full Force and Virtue. Sealed and delivered and duly stamped in the presence of:*

James Hoodless   **John Baty**   **Elizabeth Douglas**

Affidavit:

I **John Baty, of Kirkbeckstown in the Parish of Bewcastle** *in the County of Cumberland and* **James Hoodless Brampton innkeeper** *in the County of Cumberland do jointly and severally make Oath and first the said* **John Baty** *nowpaying a faculty or Licence for the Solemnization of Marriage with* **Elizabeth Douglas of Nixonstown in the Parish of Bewcastle** *in the County of Cumberland, spinster for himself maketh oath and saith that there is no lawful impediment or Lett (to the knowledge of this deponent) by reason of any pre contract, consanguinity or Affinity, but that he, this deponent and she the said* **Elizabeth Douglas** *may lawfully marry together, nor any suit, controversy or complaint moved or depending before any judge Ecclesiastical or Civil, concerning the marriage of either of them; and the said* **James Hoodless innkeeper of Brampton,** *likewise maketh Oath and Saith that he does not know of nor believes that there is any lawful Lett or impediment to obstruct or hinder their intended marriage, and that they are each above the age of one and twenty years.*

Sworn this day at Carlisle

The 25th day of November in the year of Our Lord 1751"

Fourth – Arrangements had been made for the wedding ceremony to duly take place in Stapleton Church. But, why were these plans suddenly brought forward to the **very next day: 26th November** following the signing of the marriage bond in Carlisle? What could have been the reason for such haste?

2. SOME FACTS SURROUNDING LIZZIE THE WITCH

And finally, fifth – Why was the venue suddenly changed from Scaleby Church to Brampton Church?

Brampton Church Marriage Register 1751

b) So, what might be the answers?

Peter Burn recorded that Elizabeth's brother – Captain Douglas, had greatly disapproved of Elizabeth's elopement, and, having heard of the marriage plans in Carlisle, summoned a carriage to take him to Bewcastle in order to persuade Elizabeth to give up her plans, and return with him to Castle Douglas before the marriage could take place. Peter Burn also records that the news that Captain Douglas was on his way, had reached the ears of the marriage couple and so, John Baty hastily brought forward the wedding ceremony; changed the venue to Brampton, possibly to dodge the efforts of Captain Douglas, but also to ensure that they enjoyed the legal protection of being officially married before his arrival – the consequence of which would be that Captain Douglas would have no authority to abduct his now married sister. The wedding ceremony did take place at Brampton Church on the 26th November and Captain Douglas was forced to return to Castle Douglas with an empty carriage.

2. SOME FACTS SURROUNDING LIZZIE THE WITCH

c) What happened after they got married?

Now legally married, the two settled in Bewcastle but again either mystery surrounds their lives or anecdotes surrounding the couple have been embellished over the years.

Tales were told that John had earned a living in Bewcastle as a fortune teller, but no record has ever been seen to corroborate this story. Many now believe that this is a mistake handed down in the story telling over the years and that, whereas John's professional skills as a schoolmaster would certainly be in demand, instead, it was Elizabeth who had practised the dark art of fortune telling. Further, John Baty is described on the marriage bond and again 50 years later as a "Schoolmaster" on his gravestone, which suggests that he had continued in his profession long after his marriage, whilst it is Elizabeth who is credited with having been a fortune teller in the very many anecdotes that exist in numerous reports and published items.

Peter Burn does record that Lizzie was a woman of superior education for her time and that she assisted her husband in the <u>teaching profession</u> – many daughters of the yeomen of Brampton were taught by her, particularly in the skills of knitting, sewing and housewifery. However, no record has been seen referring to John Baty practising as a school master in either Bewcastle or Brampton.

Some time later the couple left Kirkbeckstown and moved to Brampton Fell to a dwelling called Hollas or The Hollows.

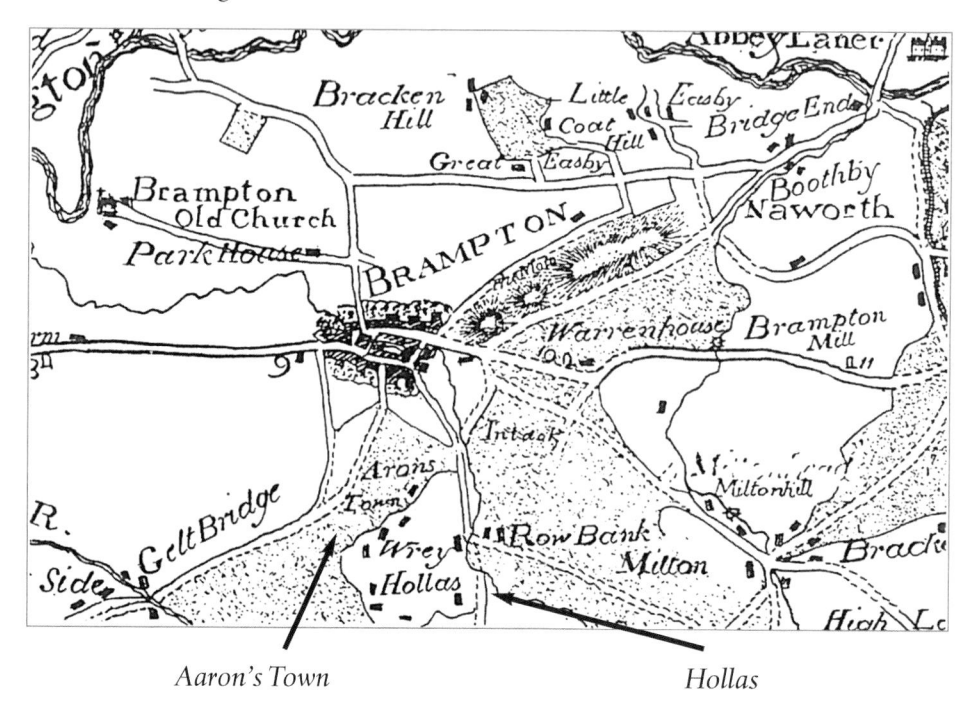

Aaron's Town   Hollas

It was here that, many years later, John died on March 30th 1808 aged 80 years. After John's death Lizzie moved to Talkin village for a short while, then to Aaron's Town in Brampton and, in her final years, to Craw Hall to a small cottage that stood near Brampton Beck in what is now the garden of Rose Villa. Lizzie's daughter – Mrs Salkeld lived quite close at Low Beckside, which at that time was called Bleach House.

Lizzie was described as a *"canny auld body"*, who usually wore a red cloak with a hood. The cloak was trimmed with white fur – a style of dress, which at the time had a stamp of respectability about it, and there is little doubt that Lizzie had enjoyed better days. Mrs Tinling confirmed that Lizzie was:

"a kind neighbourly body – ever ready to render a service."

Although she never attended a place of worship, Lizzie appears to have had a strong respect for God's word. The bible was her Sabbath reading, having a special frame on which she placed the good book whilst reading. It was said by those who wished to discredit her, that poor Lizzie looked upon such religious exercise as an insurance policy to atone for her deeds of darkness, and necromancy.

d) Lizzie's death

Lizzie's death which occurred on March 6th 1817 when she was 88 years old, was described by Mrs Tinling as *"easy"*. Lizzie had been moved from Craw Hall to her daughter's house at The Hallows and during her final hours, whilst Mrs Tinling was busy making her grave clothes, Lizzie gave instructions about the disposal of some of her property. Mrs Tinling was to have her walking stick; Joseph Parker her tea set; Mrs Gardner her chest of drawers; Mrs Johnstone of The Hollies her clay pipe, and Mr Henry Penfold her jug.

The obituary in one local newspaper was quite critical of Lizzie, suggesting that she was a fraudster:

"On Tuesday last, at Hallows, near Brampton, at an advanced age, Mrs Baty, better known by the epithet of "Old Lizzy" whose qualifications as a necromancer have for many years been celebrated by love-sick girls, nervous old maids, those who wished to find hidden treasures and others who had lost them, and by numbers of all ranks who wished to pry into the secrets of fate. But Lizzy could not only enable her applicants to take a peep into futurity, but she could even force them to Pay. The three goddesses who spin weave and cut short the destinies of us mortals, to comply with her incantations, and procure young virgins husbands according to their own wish. Mrs Baty had, no doubt, in the early part of her life been herself a consulter of fortune tellers, but her keen perception saw through the cheat; and having been first a pupil,

she next commenced mistress of the occult arts. Such are the deceptive gradations of fraud and falsehood: first we countenance the practice of them, then we are prepared to practise them ourselves."

Carlisle Journal, March 1817

The obituary in the *Carlisle Patriot* was much more kind to Lizzie:

> On Wednesday last, at Beckside, near Brampton, Mrs. Elizabeth Batey, aged 88. This old Lady was well known through this and the adjoining Counties as the Brampton Sibyl, or Witch! in which character she has practised for many years with great success, having been consulted by persons from all parts respecting stolen property and other affairs. She had also very extensive practice among the younger part of the female sex, as the expounder of their future destiny; she has frequently been consulted by persons who have come a distance of forty or fifty miles, and even more, for the sole purpose, and, as report says, her answers have been generally satisfactory. She has contrived to make a comfortable living by her profession for the greater part of her life.

Although Mrs Tinling described Lizzie's death as "easy" her funeral was certainly not so – but is surrounded like the rest of her life – by mystery and superstition. The day of Lizzie's burial at the rear of St. Martin's Church, is said to have been one of the wildest; and remembered for thunder and lightning. The report in the *Carlisle Journal* gave a graphic description of the proceedings:

"The date is March 6th 1817. It is one of the wildest days within living memory. Thunder crashes and lightning throws into momentary blinding relief the rows of tombstones in the new church graveyard. A great darkness has fallen upon Brampton and the surrounding countryside. It is so dark that the mourners at the interment have to use lanterns at the graveside. Even so, such is the strength

2. SOME FACTS SURROUNDING LIZZIE THE WITCH

of the wind that it penetrates lantern shutters, blowing out the candles so that they have to be relit again and again. The crowd at the graveside huddle together in small subdued groups. Even the brief service of burial is intoned in little above a whisper. Everyone takes the great darkness the wild rain and the incessant growling of the thunder as just another omen. During the proceedings a singular occurrence took place. A young man named Pickering, either driven by curiosity or overcome by fear, approached the lowered coffin but too near the side and accidentally slipped his foot and fell into the grave. In the coffin, now six feet below ground lies the body of no ordinary woman. It is the funeral of Lizzie Baty – the strange character known as The Brampton Witch. So Lizzie Baty was buried as she lived – surrounded by mystery and superstition."

Carlisle Journal, December 25th 1953

Or, **was** she buried? To add further to this cauldron of mystery, an interesting report of a lecture given by Alfred Sutton of Boothby "Witches and Witchcraft" to the Carlisle Scientific Society, in 1896, introduces yet more controversy to the Lizzie legacy, casting some doubt as to whether the coffin in question was actually occupied!

"A tradition still lingers locally that those who bore the coffin to the grave, solemnly affirm that it was empty and the body gone. Monstrous as this fiction seems, they believe it."

Alfred Sutton, *Carlisle Scientific Society*

It must be reasonable to believe that, being a responsible newspaper, the *Carlisle Journal's* description of the stormy events surrounding Lizzie's funeral are a true record of what actually happened. Indeed a report elsewhere in the same newspaper confirms that violent weather **did** take place that day:

"The violent storm was severely felt – the clouds seemed to open and emit torrents of liquid fire; at one moment a pitchy darkness prevailed and at the next an almost insupportable blaze illuminated the horizon."

Carlisle Journal, March 1817

And in the *Carlisle Patriot* a similar report confirms the event:

> *"On Thursday (6th March) there was a violent hurricane, accompanied with vivid lightning – the clouds seemed to emit torrents of liquid fire."*

However, we will see in a later chapter that similar stories exist of storms occurring surrounding the death of other witches both here in the Borderlands and elsewhere in England.

e) Origins of Lizzie's "Second Sight"

According to an article written by "L" in the *Carlisle Journal*, Elizabeth Douglas may well have been descended from the Black Douglases – a Highland Clan that had played a prominent part in the Pretender's invasion of England in 1715 and, having failed in their enterprise at the battle of Preston, many of the clan found it unwise to return to the highlands, and instead found refuge in the Solway area of the Borderlands. The Highland Clans were known to have believed in "Second Sight" and it is thought that Elizabeth Douglas, being the daughter of such a Highlander, had inherited the beliefs and powers of the "second sighted sawnies". An old Jacobite song refers to "Hielanders" and "Second Sighted Sawnies":

> *"Will they a' come back to their ain dear glen?*
> *Will they a come back these Hielanmen?*
> *Second sighted Sawnie she looked fu' wae*
> *And mithers they grat as they marched awa*
> *Wi a hundred pipers an ' a' an' a'."*

A "Douglas" is certainly listed among those who fought at Preston and later escaped to Scotland.

f) Lizzie and Religion

Elizabeth Baty was believed by some Brampton folk to have sold herself to the devil, yet Mrs Tinling referred to Lizzie as:

2. SOME FACTS SURROUNDING LIZZIE THE WITCH

"a kind and neighbourly body who although never attended a place of worship, appeared to have a strong regard for god's word – the bible was her Sabbath reading having a special frame on which she placed the good book whilst reading."

There is further evidence of Lizzie's belief in religion, in her own admission to Mrs Tinling that, shortly after having eloped, she had spent some time on her knees praying above a grave in a churchyard, in an attempt to assuage her anxieties over the wisdom of her actions. Furthermore, many anecdotes refer to her efforts in assisting those who had suffered loss, and the fear that wrongdoers had of becoming the victim of one of her curses. Some of her contemporaries described Lizzie as having a strange mixture of religion and superstition. She was certainly a woman with a strong personality, gaining much respect from most people, but from others, a great degree of fear. Stories exist of her willingness to assist folk in trouble, whilst others believed that she took advantage of the superstitions of simple folk prevalent at the time and benefited financially from their eager requests for help.

Many anecdotes refer to Lizzie as *"a terror to evil doers"*. It was believed that she had powers over such people: if when some article or other had been stolen and the thief heard that the person who had lost the items had visited Lizzie, the thief would become so terrified of becoming the recipient of a curse, that they restored the stolen items to the owner. Honest people therefore, had great faith in Lizzie, whilst wrongdoers lived in fear of her curses. Others believed that Lizzie possessed magic powers and sought after her for advice on curing various ailments or afflictions. Some claimed that she was a soothsayer, reading people's hands and forecasting their future. In particular she had earned a reputation for helping people to find articles that had become lost.

Doctor Faustus – a play by Christopher Marlow at the time of Shakespeare, tells the story of a well respected scholar and doctor, who, having grown dissatisfied with the pursuit of knowledge, agreed to a deal by signing up with his blood to serve the devil in exchange for acquiring the skills and practice of necromancy, magic, the black arts, and the ability of conjuring up visions. The price to be paid for this contract was that on his death, Dr Faustus' soul would descend into the permanent horrors of Hell.

Upon his death Dr Faustus' soul is carried off by a host of devils accompanied by lightning, fire and tempest – just like the circumstances accompanying Lizzie's interment. Many of Dr Faustus' activities have a striking resemblance to some of those attributed to Lizzie Baty and, in particular, the events which really did take place at her funeral.

Having established some of the facts surrounding Lizzie's life, we can now retell the stories attributed to her, and later, consider if they could possibly be true.

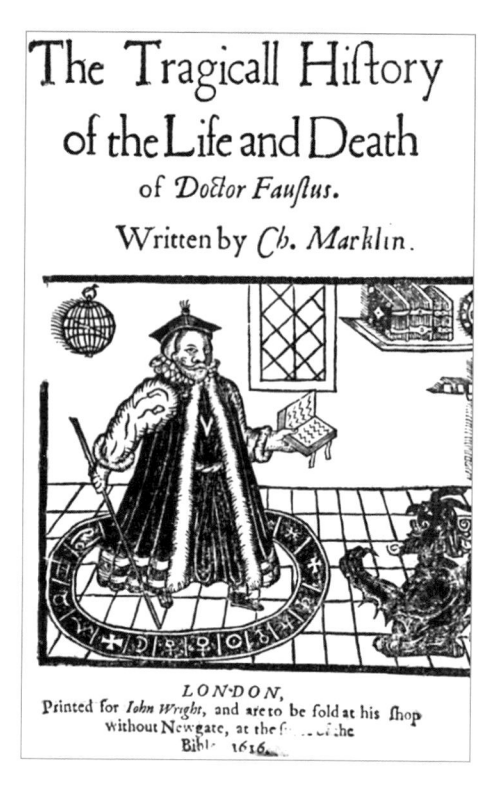

In the meantime take care not to walk under any ladders, and – look out for black cats.

Chapter 3

LOCAL STORIES ATTRIBUTED TO LIZZIE THE WITCH

a) The stolen spade

An old man of 75 years living two miles away from Brampton had a spade stolen from his garden. He went to Lizzie at once and she told him to return home and walk towards a moorland part, some three to four miles from his home, telling him to take this turn and that turn until he came to a gate. From this gate, he would see a thorn bush at a certain distance, and in that thorn bush he would find his spade concealed. The old man, knowing every inch of the road and the thorn bush mentioned by Lizzie, returned home; went to the thorn bush ... and found his spade!

b) The market Stallholder

A market stallholder in Brampton stopped supplying Lizzie with her rations of butter, and a short while after, the stallholder found that she could not get her lard to set, and worse still, Lizzie predicted that the stall holder's daughter who was shortly to get married:

> *"would get a white dress sooner."*

The white dress turned out to be a funeral gown.

c) The end of presents from a farmer's wife

Mrs G., a farmer's wife, lived in the neighbourhood of Carlisle, and was moved to visit Lizzie to make her presents of butter, eggs and other farm produce. However, the farmer's wife was unable to continue the good will and discontinued her visits. Shortly after, ill luck befell the farmer's wife. The horse that had carried her to and from Brampton sickened and died; the butter failed to churn properly; cream bowls were broken and similar disasters began to occur daily. In her distress, the farmer's wife consulted a priest who advised her to break the spell by visiting Lizzie once more, and to draw blood from her. The farmer's wife came to Lizzie's cottage and before Lizzie was aware of her intention, the farmer's wife drew a darning needle from her pocket and wounded Lizzie on the forehead. This scene was witnessed by a Mrs Rutherford who reported the assault. The farmer's wife was, however none the better for her visit, as a short while after, she threw herself into a well where she drowned.

d) Restoration of lost articles

Mrs L. had on several occasions lost the butter that she had bought at Brampton market, and matters became worse when she also lost a leg of lamb. Mrs L. visited Lizzie to seek the name of the thief. Lizzie, after careful thought, declared that Mrs L.'s suspicions were ill founded – that no thief was involved but that a Spaniel dog, belonging to Captain Oliver, was the culprit. Lizzie also advised that in addition a wedge of soap had also been carried off. Further advice was given in that Mrs L. should go to a midden in the brewery field where she would find the wedge of soap and the remains of the leg of lamb. Mrs L. did as she was advised and found the articles as described.

e) Forecasting a marriage

Two young teenage girls decided to visit Lizzie to have their fortunes told. One of the teenagers asked Lizzie about who she would marry, to which Lizzie is reported as having replied:

> "Thou needn't bother the sell aboot a wedding sweetheart; and I say thou'll git a white dress soon enough."

Both teenagers were at a loss as to what to make of Lizzie's predictions. On the Tuesday following, whilst one of the young women was hanging out the washing, she caught a cold which developed into a fever leading to her death. The young girl's white dress turned out to be a shroud.

f) Forecasting another marriage

Another two girls wishing to know which of them would be lucky enough to marry a certain gentleman, set out from Carlisle to Brampton to consult Lizzie over which of them would marry. The journey was long and wearisome. On reaching Warwick Bridge one girl said to the other:

> "What can that Old bitch tell us? I am going back."

The other girl persevered and continued on to Brampton to see the old woman, and finally arriving in Craw Hall, knocked at Lizzie's door. The witch opened the door but before the girl could explain the reason for her visit, Lizzie burst out:

> "An where's yer friend? And what can an Old bitch like me tell you?"

Whereupon Lizzie slammed the door shut.

g) A deceitful coalman

According to a Mrs Rutherford, Lizzie, with others, had ordered a cartload of coal. The cartman had been fortunate in procuring some good quality coal which he intended taking to his favourite customer elsewhere in Brampton. However, when opposite Lizzie's front door, the horse stopped, and in spite of being urged on with whip and shouts, the horse refused to go further. Wearied at length by his efforts to move the horse, the cartman turned into Lizzie's house and informed her that he had brought her a load of good coals. Lizzie's reply was:

> "Nae thanks to thee! If the hoss hadn't mair sense then its maister, I wadn't hae gitten them."

h) A curse on two girls

Two girls who lived at Hemblesgate Farm had a pet lamb. One day, as they happened to be standing at the door of their farmhouse watching their pet lamb jumping around, "Ole Lizzie" came past their door on her way home to Craw Hall. Dressed in her usual red cloak, the pet lamb ran up to Lizzie, butted her legs and knocked her over. The young girls, much amused by the incident, never attempted to come to Lizzie's rescue, and both laughed heartily at Lizzie's misfortune. Lizzie, being quite annoyed at the girls' enjoyment and uncaring attitude said:

> *"Aye aye ye've enjoyed yersells an hed a good laugh at my expense. Ye shall hae plenty o laughing an dancing efter this I tell ye."*

Hemblesgate Farm (Hemmels Yett)

The two girls on entering the farm began to behave *"with maniacal manoeuvres and became quite mad"*.

> *"They danc'd an danc'd like mad they danc'd*
> *An sair the neighbours fret*
> *Twas said the devil led off the reel*
> *That neet at Hemmel's yet."*

This behaviour continued for several days despite the girls' parents offering gifts to Lizzie. The local vicar was consulted and advised pushing nine pins into the ground in order to obtain liberty. Meanwhile Lizzie had become quite busy with requests for consultations from a number of other "customers" and whilst her attention was focused on counting her money, the nine pins appear to have broken the spell:

Peter Burn's poem "Lizzie Baty" composed in 1864 retells the incident in local dialect:

LIZZIE BATY

Twee lassies full o' fun,
Mak mirth at lizzie's fright;
A dumpy wally, meddl'd wi'
Hes shown the lady fright.
An her distress ye weel may guess
For sair her pride is stung-
The twee are promised their deserts,
In her prophetic tongue
"o ye may dance ye're mocking dance,
An giggle to ye're will,
This witch wife works ye fun eneuf.
An ye shall hae yer fill."
The little toon is a'stir
The lasses laugh an'rin,
The clapper I'the Applegarth

B. Scott & Son, Carlisle.

*Yours truly,
Peter Burn*

3. LOCAL STORIES ATTRIBUTED TO LIZZIE THE WITCH

Mak's nit a bigger din
Alang the delf rack dance they noo,
An'plates gae click a clack,
The mice are match'd for nimbleness,
An ken na what tae think.
Sae loud they laugh – therir voices rin,
Like an alarm clock,
The crazy strain tak's cock and hen,
An dog an' bubbling jock.
They danc'd an danc'd like mad they danc'd
An sair the nehbors fret,
Twas said the deil led off the reel,
That neet at Hemmel's Yet.
O weary days an'weary nights,
The young folk hed to bide,
An news o' Lizzie's witchery,
Hes travell'd far an wide.
There cam that great a holy man,
Weel skilled in sec like art;
O'him they seek a kindly help
To gar the spell depart.
I hae nea power to brek the spell,
I can but neame its kind-
Nine pins deep driven I'the ground,
The bonnie lasses bind.
Ilk day and night the witch wife gaes,
An shifts ilk siller pin,
An while she plies her idle task,
The twee mun dance and grin.
Should she forget 'mang other work,
The shifting o'ilk pin;
The lasses shall hae liberty;
To mingle wi their kin,

They wait an wail
Mebbe she may forget!
But aye thery dance an dance an ae they laugh
The dame's no sleeping yet.
But Lizzier as a busy time,
Wi' strangers that can pay.
An moments strung wi siller coins
Can pleasant music play.
An clink a clink the money goes,
As roun an roun it spins.
Wi busy watchin o'the coins
She quite forgets the pins.
A queen can nobbut hod the reins
Till fortune gaes a pitch
Our lady's thrown – the spell undone,
Gaes freedom frae te witch,
An lang the lasses leeve to tell,
To nehbor an to kin
How Lizzie wi'her witchery,
Hed gar'd them dance an grin.

i) A cottager loses his meat – and also his courage

A further story – somewhat difficult to believe, is recorded, again involving stolen articles. A humble cottager of Brampton kept a pig, which he killed just before Christmas in order to sell the meat. The hams he sold green to help pay his rent, the sides he laid down in salt to cure for his own family's use, and placed them in an outhouse. When the time arrived for hanging them up in the kitchen to dry, to his dismay, he found that they had been stolen. As soon as his day's work was finished he set off to Craw Hall, not to consult the constable or solicitor, but to confer with "Ole Lizzie".

As soon as she had heard his melancholy tale, Lizzie enquired of the cottager:

"Would you like to see the man who has stolen your flecks o bacon?"

The poor fellow replied: *"That's just what I have come for"* to which Lizzie next said:

"Sit theesell doon theer then."

Pointing to a chair just inside the door of her room, the cottager readily obeyed and as soon as he was seated, Lizzie rose up, cleared the centre of the room, blew out the candle and took into her hand a white wand, with which she drew a circle upon the floor. No sooner had she drawn this circle than a great light filled the room, and, to the poor cottager's great consternation, he saw the figure of a man come up through the floor in the very centre of the circle with the two stolen flecks of bacon on his back. Did the poor cottager collar him and recover his bacon? – alas no! He immediately jumped out of the chair, terrified and exclaiming:

"For God's sake let him gan, bacon an aa an let me oot o this hoose."

Whereupon he rushed out of the house never stopping his flight, till he got home.

j) Restoration of stolen property

About 1810 a farmer's daughter, having been a pupil of Lizzie and whose family had moved from Brampton to Wigton, had several geese stolen from her new farm. An uncle of the farmer's daughter who had great faith in Lizzie's occult powers asked his niece to visit Lizzie in Brampton in order to find out who had stolen the geese. With little intention of obeying this request the young lady did visit Brampton and called upon Lizzie but instead asked for her fortune to be told. Lizzie got the cards out and told her fortune in the old fashioned and orthodox way. This done, the young lady spoke of leaving as it was beginning to get dark, when Lizzie remarked:

"You surely are not ganning yet – hadn't thou something to ask me aboot?"

In reply, the young woman said:

"Well if you know that I had something to ask you about, you'll know what it is."

To which Lizzie responded:

"Wasn't it something to do about geese?"

On hearing this, the young woman, having forgotten all about the geese felt her hair rising at the back of her head with fear. Lizzie went on to say that in addition to losing the geese something else had now been stolen, and that upon her return home she should advise her father to keep his stable better locked. When the young lady got home the discovery was made that a new saddle and bridle had been stolen from the stable. Lizzie indicated later who the thief was.

k) Restoration of stolen money

A clerk, was one day, returning to Kirkhouse from Brampton with a bag of cash to pay the workmen's wages, when he was waylaid on the road in daylight by robbers and relieved of the money. On hearing about the events, an official from the workplace went to Lizzie to ask for help. Lizzie instructed her client to go to a certain spot at Talkin Tarn where he would find a peat stack. Lizzie assured the official that he would find the missing money on the East side of the stack quoting the exact number of peats from the bottom, and from the South side where he would find a loose peat behind which was the money. Lizzie's prediction turned out to be accurate and the money was found intact.

l) A farmer's wife fails to make her butter

A farmer's wife in Milton regularly provided butter for the table from the churning of the milk from her cows and Lizzie was a grateful recipient of the occasional gift:

"... just to keep on the right side of her."

Unfortunately, for a short period, the milk refused to turn into butter, despite lengthy churning and Lizzie was thought to have cast a spell upon the dairy.

After consulting a wise man, advice was given to use a stick made from a rowan tree to churn the milk. Thereafter butter came regularly and Lizzie once more had butter on the table.

m) A poor woman is snubbed by Lizzie
A poor woman living in Etterby, Carlisle, one day, had her weekly washing stolen whilst it was hanging out to dry, and, in distress and dismay, having consulted her neighbours, was advised to go to Brampton to visit Lizzie Baty suggesting that:

> "Ole Lizzie will soon tell you who has stolen yer clothes."

The disconsolate old woman impatiently replied somewhat disparagingly:

> "Tut, what can that ole witch tell us aboot it?"

However, the old lady was eventually persuaded to go, and when she reached Brampton, she nervously entered Lizzie's house finding Lizzie sitting on her customary chair in the corner of the room. Before her visitor had time to utter a word about her plight, Lizzie announced:

> "Ye can gan all yer way back again for the ole witch will tell you nothing about what you have come to ask her aboot."

n) Lizzie conjures up a transformation

> "Old Mr W. and a few friends, accompanied by hounds, went for a day's hunting on Haltwhistle Fell. Mid day was reached without their having had a run. Tired and disheartened, they came to Four Lonning Ends and there espied Lizzie. *To the Branton Witch we owe our ill luck today! Let us run her down!*" came the cry. The cry was immediately taken up and the chase begun. But Lizzie stole a march upon them, by turning herself into a hare, and started off for home. They pursued her over

Haltwhistle Fell, through Talkin village, then to Old Beck Side and down Craw Hall Lonning. Here the hare, taking advantage of a hole in a cottage door entered, and disappeared. The hunters, aggravated by their defeat, broke open the door, entered the room to find Lizzie in bed with a scratched leg!"

Howsonian Advertiser, April 1960

This account is quite different from all of the other stories referring to Lizzie, in that it refers to a transformation i.e. turning herself into a hare and then reforming herself after reaching her house. Whilst other stories credited to Lizzie's actions might almost be credible to some "believers", the hare story does take some believing and most people would consider it pure invention.

o) A farmer's wife refuses to sell a black hen to Lizzie and pays for her mistake

"Ole Lizzie" wandered about the countryside and was always a welcome guest wherever she went, mostly respected for her powers. One night, on her way home to Brampton, after one of her customary perambulations, she called at the house of a farmer at Talkin. She was kindly welcomed, placed in the warmest seat in the chimney corner and hospitably entertained. Eventually as she rose to leave she enquired of the farmer's wife if she would sell her a certain black hen which the farmer's wife had amongst her poultry. The answer came:

> *"No I won't sell the black hen as she is laying at the moment and the only one I have that is laying – but I will sell you any of the others."*

On hearing this Lizzie replied:

> *"Varra weel, say nay mair aboot it."*

She left the house very abruptly, apparently much annoyed. As soon as the husband thought that Lizzie had got beyond earshot he whispered to his wife:

> *"Why didn't yer let her hev the black hen? She'll raise the win' afore the morning and do us a mischief."*

The wind certainly did rise that night, tearing off much of the thatched roof, allowing the rain to pour heavily into their bedroom, soaking the farmer and his wife.

p) Lizzie casts a curse upon an unhelpful landlord/innkeeper

Samuel Stephenson, landlord and innkeeper at the Wellington public house on the Sands in Brampton, was out delivering orders of whisky, to clients by horse and cart along Craw Hall. Lizzie on seeing the deliveries, asked Samuel Stephenson for some of the whisky … which he refused. Later that day, on one of his delivery stops, Samuel Stephenson's cart over balanced and all of the containers of whisky tumbled to the ground and smashed, spilling their contents onto the street.

q) The Tea set of Lizzie Baty

A report in the *Cumberland News* of 2010 adds further mystery to Lizzie's legacy:

> *"In 1817 a mysterious old woman known of as the Brampton Witch gifted her set of china to a local friend on her death bed. Builder/joiner and undertaker Joseph Parker was in the habit of assisting Lizzie when times were hard for her. Later, at the age of 88 years Lizzie summoned John Parker to her cottage at Craw Hall in her dying hours and as a token of her appreciation of his kindness to her, she gave him the tea set, but according to legend, the gift was accompanied by a spell. The spell amounted to the threat that any member of the family of the person drinking from the cups would be visited by good luck. However, the spell also threatened that if the china were to leave the Parker family it would be the harbinger of disaster for the new owner."*

Now, nearly 200 years later, the antique china is still in mint condition and has been handed down, carefully through the generations of the Parker family. After Joseph's death the tea set was handed down to his daughter Frances, who later married to become Frances Bell of Main Street Brampton, and later to John Parker's great niece Mary – all of whom have said that the mystery of the cursed tea set has gripped the family with apprehension and sometimes fear. The infamous tea set eventually passed down the family to Mary's daughter Marion Reed. Jim Parker Templeton, Marion's son, felt that he owed his life to the superstition associated with the tea set.

Jim grew up listening to the tales about the Brampton Witch; about her predictions for the future and to the grisly fate that awaited those who offended her. When war was declared in 1939, Jim was in one of the first groups of young men called up to fight. But, before he left for duty, Marion, his mother, sent him to seek out some good luck.

> *"She told me to cycle from our home in Carlisle to a family member's house in Brampton to drink a cup of tea from the china. At that time I was not convinced but did it because I was told to do so."*

Just days after, Jim joined the Royal Army Medical Corps with whom he stayed until the end of the war in 1945. But, of the 500 men sent to fight with him, Jim was one of only 37 who returned:

3. LOCAL STORIES ATTRIBUTED TO LIZZIE THE WITCH

"We lost most men in the battle of Salerno, in Southern Italy. I would get these feelings as if I was being prompted to move – so I did – and then something would land on the place where I had been standing – a shell."

After the war Jim married Annie and was father of three daughters. None of the family was keen to take responsibility for the china for fear of the consequences and it was handed over to a Parker within the extended family. Jim Templeton also tells the tale that when his mother Marion was dying, she said to Jim:

"You will see my coffin three times... ."

After her death she was buried in the family grave in Brampton church yard, but the following day there was a landslide, exposing the coffin which had to be buried a second time. The coffin was buried again, but a mistake was made by the gravedigger as he had not placed Mary's uncle's coffin beneath hers as it should have been. Both coffins were then disinterred and then re-interred in the correct order. The prophesy of seeing her coffin three times turned out to be a reality!

Chapter 4

WITCHCRAFT: A DARK ART?

The era in which we now live has seen considerable change, the consequence of which is that old customs, old beliefs, old superstitions and sayings which had been the bedrock of our forefathers' culture, have largely disappeared. However, still today, there linger in the minds of some people, the embers of beliefs about bad luck; curses; the causes of unusual events; and the paranormal.

Witchcraft continues to keep its hold on the minds of a small body of "believers"; on many who are unsure, but who wish to keep an open mind, and of peasants and simple folk.

According to M.S. Wilkie in his book *Border customs and superstitions*, a horse shoe nailed upon, or above a door ensures the exclusion of a witch. Many an upturned horse shoe or rusty sickle can be found hanging on front doors, sheds and stables in the Brampton area – is this just an innocent expression or hopeful insurance against bad luck?

Of Lizzie, not one of her neighbours ever dared to offend her openly, or if she at any time sought a request, it would be granted for fear of a curse being placed upon the unfortunate recipient. For those who did refuse a request, and those who spoke ill of her, there are plenty of anecdotes of the misery that they are alleged to have suffered as a result.

Chapter 5

... OR A CONFIDENCE TRICK?

Some historians claim that White witches or wise women were confidence tricksters who were well educated or of high intelligence and who made a good living by taking advantage of the beliefs of simple country folk. By careful interrogation of their customer, wise women could often be able to draw conclusions and give advice on certain courses of action – rather like today's Management Consultants! Several stories refer to young girls travelling to consult Lizzie over whom they would marry. Whenever such a person sought advice on the selection of a suitor from the number of her admirers, Lizzie would use the practice of "Bible and Key" to assist in arriving at the solution. First, Lizzie would spend some considerable time chatting to the girl about her admirers, and in that process, would quietly assess from the girl's responses which of her suitors she most admired. Then, having opened up the Bible at The Book Of Ruth which includes the phrase *"Whither Thou goest then I will follow"*, and placing the key upon that page, Lizzie would then close the Bible and bind it with string, the two ends of which would be held in the little fingers of each of Lizzie's hands. The girl would then be asked to name one of her admirers and if the key remained in its position then that name would count as a rejection, and the next name would be called out by the girl. At some stage after a name had been called out, the Bible would suddenly turn over and the key drop out – this being a sure sign of the person to whom she would be married.

It must be noted, however, that at all times, it would be Lizzie who would be in charge of holding the strings, and no doubt she would manipulate the Bible to turn when the name of the assumed preferred admirer was called out.

Many of the stories in Chapter 2 follow similar stories of witches elsewhere and encourage the view that most of them could be pure invention, handed down by story tellers feeding the imaginations of receptive audiences, whilst other accounts firmly claim that such events really did take place and were personally witnessed.

There are common themes which flow constantly through many witch stories across the regions of United Kingdom and of Europe and show a striking resemblance to those stories accredited to Lizzie Baty of Brampton.

Lizzie conjures up a storm

In Chapter 2, a report in the *Carlisle Journal* records the dramatic events surrounding the interment of Lizzie Baty at Brampton church graveyard in 1817. It is reasonable to believe that the *Carlisle Journal* being a responsible newspaper, the report would be an accurate record of what took place, and indeed the local weather report confirms that such a storm did take place; however there is a suspicious and remarkable similarity surrounding the deaths of other witches.

Beth Chambers, the witch of Workington who died in 1839 had predicted that her death:

"will be accompanied by a great wind, and that everything will go strange."

The following day a great storm blew up and on visiting Beth's house, neighbours found her, not only dead, but already dressed in a shroud ready for burial. No one locally admitted to *"laying her out"*.

According to Anthony Whitehead's book of 1896 *Legends of Westmorland*, Mary Barnes, the witch of Tebay, caused many injuries to her neighbours and could raise storms. She was believed to have sold herself to the devil, and that at her death, a great storm arose which, it is claimed, carried her off to Hell.

According to an article in *The News* of December 17th 1921 by a Mrs J. Allsopp, Nanny the Witch of Denton – just a few miles east of Brampton was also reputed to have been accompanied by immense thunderstorms at her burial in the old church yard at Denton:

"at Denton on the day that Nanny died, there was a most awful thunderstorm ever known in these parts. The lightning ran along the ground and the thunder was terrible."

Lizzie casts a spell on two young girls

The account of Lizzie casting a spell upon two young girls who laughed at Lizzie's misfortune is very similar to a story appearing in a local newspaper. In her article in *The News* December 1821, Mrs J. Allsopp claims that:

"... it happened on the day that Nanny The Denton Witch was going past a farm where the maidens were washing in the open air. As she passed, the girls laughed at her ugliness, to which Nanny remonstrated ... 'Ye may laugh and dance till I choose ye ter stop'.

Immediately they began to laugh and dance uncontrollably and nothing could stop them. At last in desperation, their master went to the old witch and prayed on bended knees in front of her asking for forgiveness. This she did – only after they had danced for 24 hours."

Lizzie transforms herself into a hare

The story of Lizzie Baty transforming herself into a hare whilst being chased by unsuccessful hunters on Haltwhistle Moor (Chapter 2) also has remarkable similarities with other witch stories.

A witch living in Hawkwell, Northumberland, is reported as having transformed herself into a hare, and after causing mischief, escaped by bolting through a trap hole in a door when being chased.

And again, high up in Eskdale was a hare that escaped all hounds in the chase. However, one day a black dog cornered the hare during a hunt. The hare turned to a stone wall and attempted escape through a "smout" or sheephole. Just as the hare reached the hole, the dog caught it by the back leg but was unable to hold fast on it. The hare escaped and the huntsmen, being suspicious, later called upon the witch of Eskdale to report their findings – and found her in bed, injured. The witch claimed that she had fallen earlier that day, but the wound looked very much like a dog bite.

H.S. Cowper in his book *Cumbrian Folklore* tells a similar story: in the village of Outgate near Hawkshead, the local hounds were in full pursuit of a hare, whilst hunting in the valley, and chased it into the hamlet making straight for a house, where it jumped through an open window, but was caught by the hind leg by one of the hounds. At the same time, there came from within the house a wild screaming. The huntsmen gathered around the house and on gaining entry, they found no hare but the notorious Witch of Outgate.

The witch of Guisborough was said to be lame for years – the wounds having been received from a dog which bit her whilst she was slipping through a hole in her own front door following a hunt.

Thomas Gibson in his book *Legends and historical notes on Places in North Westmorland* records the exploits of Mary Barnes the Tebay witch:

"A legend occurs that an old woman who resided at Tebay could turn herself into the form of a hare, and in this state used to give sport and much trouble to the dogs of a neighbouring squire who could never catch her. The old witch prophesied that carriages without horses would one day run over the fells – this was later turned into reality when the Lancaster and Carlisle Railway constructed a rail line over which horseless carriages were hauled."

Thomas Gibson

In his research, Thomas Gibson refers to *"shape shifting and prophetic declarations"* as being traditional characteristics of witch stories during the 18th century.

Thomas Wilson, a Northumberland miner and poet, in his anthology of 1843 *The Pitman's Pay and other poems* describes a hunt which is believed to have taken place where the old witch also turned herself into a hare. The origins of this account of Lizzie the witch, may lay in the imaginations of local Brampton people who might have invented this legend having heard of Mary Barnes the witch of Tebay.

Sir Walter Scott refers to witches exchanging their form with hares:

"Hare, hare, God send thee care
I am in a hare's likeness now
But I shall be a woman even now
Hare, hare, god send thee care."
                    Walter Scott Sir, *Demonology and Witchcraft*

The hare theme appears in witch stories in virtually every rural area throughout the United Kingdom.

Lizzie has "second sight"

Lizzie was consulted by two young girls wanting to have their fortunes told and in particular who they might marry. To one of the girls she replied:

"Thou needn't bother thysell aboot a wedding – thou'll get a white dress soon enough."

The young girl, a short while later, caught a cold whilst hanging out the washing which developed into a fever and death. The white dress forecast by Lizzie was a shroud. Second sight featuring death is a common theme in Northumberland and the Scottish Highlands. Whilst visiting the witch of Belsay, a shepherd sought advice concerning an ill sheep. The witch advised him to forget about the sheep as another death was more imminent.

Joan Wyatt the witch of Bodmin in 1775 was reported as having predicted a birth, a marriage and a death.

Lizzie's blood breaks a spell
Mrs G. a farmer's wife pierced Lizzie's skin with a needle in order to break a spell that she believed was responsible for a series of bad luck incidents. Drawing blood from a witch was thought to be a sure way of breaking a curse or spell, and features in other witch stories. In 1672, Thomas Denton, Justice of the Peace in Carlisle, heard several charges against Elizabeth Howe of Thursby, and accused her of being:

> *"a person of evil life doing many injuries to her neighbours by witchcraft and evil arts."*

She was accused of causing a horse to die following an argument with its owner; of predicting the illness and death of another neighbour's cow, and of placing a curse on a brother and sister resulting in both of them becoming seriously ill. Having received advice that the curse could be lifted by "blooding the witch", Elizabeth Howe was invited into the house of the brother and sister, where the witch was set upon and cut with a knife. Blood flowing freely from the wound appears to have solved the problem – shortly after the brother and sister:

> *"found great ease of their torments."*

In the village of Cheriton Bishop near Exeter, the cause of a young girl's sudden illness was considered to be the work of the local witch. Seizing an opportunity when the witch was alone and unprotected, the parents of the young girl scratched the witch with a nail, allowing the blood to flow – the girl later recovered.

In his book *Folklore of the Northern Counties*, William Henderson refers to drawing blood above the mouth from the person who had caused the witchery, as the preferred method of breaking a spell. A cow belonging to a tenant farmer of Belsay suffered a broken leg; a calf died, and a horse got stuck. The farmer believing that a spell had been cast upon his farm, was advised by a skilled person to draw blood from the witch. The following day the farmer chose to cause an argument with the witch and in the process assaulted her by scratching her face. A short while later no further accidents occurred on the farm.

Mr J.—— of Halifax claimed, that an old man he knew well, was said to have undertaken the very dangerous task of catching the witch of Halifax and drawing blood from her. This he did by striking her with a three pronged table fork when he visited her house. The following morning the old witch woman became ill in bed where she remained for several days, whilst the person upon whom a spell had been cast, was relieved of all troubles.

A further blood letting story is claimed to have taken place in Framwellgate. In 1868 a family assaulted the witch of the village of Pity Me who had bewitched their daughter. Again, advice was sought from a wise man who suggested that they seize the old lady by the arm, wound her till it bled, whereupon the spell would be broken.

Finally – and this one is very difficult to believe – in 1870 a man in Barnstaple scratched the arm of a young girl with a needle, believing her to have cast a spell, whereby he had lost 14 canaries and 50 goldfinches.

Lizzie restores lost and stolen property

Mrs L. who lost a leg of lamb was advised by Lizzie that the lost/stolen property could be found in a midden, and a 75 year old man was similarly advised by Lizzie that his stolen spade could be found hidden in a bush: in each case giving precise information where the objects could be found.

Similar stories of the recovery of lost property occur in other witch stories in North England. A miller named William L.—— lost a set of new weights very mysteriously, and after exhaustive searches and inquiries, decided to consult the Witch of Stokesley. After stating his case, the witch announced that the miller could easily find the missing items by searching in the midden, and that is where they were recovered. It is interesting also to note that in both cases the lost or stolen articles had been recovered from a midden!

Lizzie has foresight or is it clairvoyance?

Two stories exist whereby Lizzie is claimed to have known before the knock came to her door, the reason why a person had arrived to seek advice. Two girls wishing to know the names of the men that they would marry decided to visit Lizzie, but at Warwick Bridge, one of them turned back believing their visit would be a waste of time, claiming *"What could that old bitch tell us anyway?"* On opening the door to the remaining girl, Lizzie immediately asked her *"and where is yer friend? And what can an old bitch tell you"* whereupon the door was slammed in the girl's face.

Similar stories exist of witches elsewhere having foresight: a man of Danby had a cow which fell ill with disease, and decided to consult the local witch. Arriving at the witch's house and on opening the door, before he had time to explain his errand the witch said: *"I know what has brought you here, you have come about an ill cow."*

Mrs J. Allsopp records that in the 1820s Nanny the Witch of Denton village had the power to inflict ill will and to foresee events. Local people went in fear of her but were also keen to consult her when things went missing or lost – a dairyman was concerned that several of his butter firkins went missing and feared that they had been stolen. Although reluctant to consult the witch for advice, he finally agreed to visit her with his neighbour for support. As they approached her dwelling, Nanny came out of her house and called over to the visitors:

"Do not come any further, the man who has your firkins is with you."

...and, it turned out to be true.

Lizzie casts a spell to stop the butter

The story of the farmer's wife at Milton, whose butter refused to arrive during churning, because of a wicked spell from Lizzie the Witch, is similar to several other recorded tales using Rowan wood to rectify the situation. One of the most common accusations of witches in the countryside was to hinder the dairy maid or cows in the making of butter. Such stories are told in North Yorkshire, Durham, Cumberland and Northumberland of butter refusing to form despite endless churning, and the local witch is blamed for having cast a spell.

Dairy maids in the village of Mallerstang – and others – used a Rowan tree branch to stir the cream and make butter, free from the enchantment of the Mallerstang Witch.

5. ... OR A CONFIDENCE TRICK?

In Devonshire, a dairymaid ran to her mistress to declare:

"Please Mam to send someone else to make butter – I have been stirring the cream ever so long but the butter will not come – and I fear it to be bewitched."

The mistress gave instructions to cut twigs from a Rowan bush and set them alight against the wall of the dairy which rescued the situation.

Milk at Nibthwaite Grange in Westmorland was considered bewitched as it would not turn to butter despite many hours of churning – the witch of Coniston being charged with having cast a spell following some harsh words from the local Squire.

Chapter 6

SO, TRUE OR FALSE?

Some will be surprised to find that a witch story they had thought belonged exclusively to Brampton, can also be readily found elsewhere. Such common themes as the hare story, and predicting the whereabouts of lost or stolen objects appear across many rural regions, not only of the United Kingdom but also of Europe, and are referred to by folklore researchers, as "migratory legends".

Many would dismiss the stories as folklore, pure phantasy, fiction: the invention of story tellers wishing to entertain. Yet can we be entirely sure? Might there be at least a vestige of truth in some of these wild fanciful stories? Records certainly exist in Brampton, of several people claiming to have witnessed some of the events described in the Lizzie stories. However, modern theory now suggests that if the same story appears elsewhere, told by other persons and of other places, then it is hard to believe that the same thing really did happen.

Chapter 7

WITCHCRAFT OVER THE CENTURIES

In very early times of our civilised world, belief in witchcraft was strongly held across many cultures and still lingers today in some remote areas of the world and in groups of believers within our modern society. Belief in the evil powers was once universal throughout Christendom and our Borderlands were no exception – especially on the Scottish side.

Celtic Society

Witchcraft certainly existed in early Celtic society – but not as today's stereotyped figure in black with a conical hat and black cat. The Celtic witch was an accepted member of the community, functioning as a healer, a physician, a predictor of future events. Historians describe such people as "White Witches" i.e. they were considered to be benevolent to the community in which they lived. White witches were considered to be "Wise Women" to whom folk would turn to for advice in family matters, in health issues – both for themselves and their livestock, in attempting to understand unforeseen events, failed harvests, and how to protect themselves from evil forces. Wise Women became important members of the community, in great demand and could earn a steady living.

Later, and in order to maintain their status in the community, many witches developed elaborate and mysterious rituals – partly to create and nourish a belief in their "magic" and the supernatural, and partly to impress their hapless victims. The development of such ritualistic behaviours led to a transition away from the popular beliefs of the usefulness of witches, to a less trusted role as a summoner of evil spirits to do harm to others. Historians consider this group to be "Black Witches" i.e. considered to be harmful and malevolent to the community in which they lived. Such transition led to the Medieval Church adopting powers to punish Black witches for having dabbled in magic or sorcery, believing them to have been taken over by the devil. Pope Innocent VIII in 1484 deemed witchcraft as heresy and gave authority to priests to cast out the devil by means of the most appalling torture – of burning and hanging.

1486 Malleus Maleficarum

In 1486 two German monks published a witch hunting manual called *Malleus Maleficarum*.

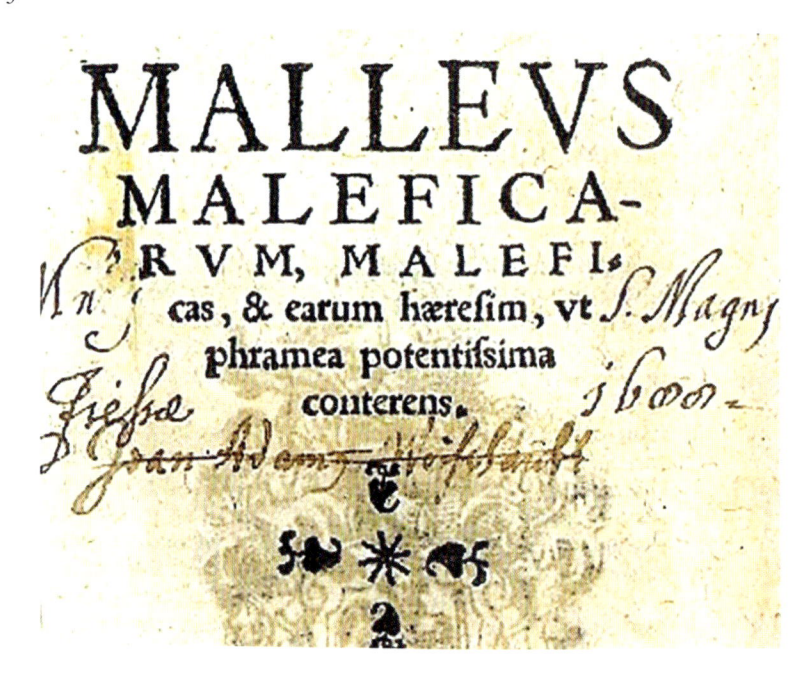

This instruction manual *How to hammer witches* showed how to identify a witch, how to conduct a witch trial, and how to administer the recommended types of punishment, and served as the standard guidance for dealing with witches throughout the Renaissance period.

7. WITCHCRAFT OVER THE CENTURIES

1541 Witchcraft in England

In 1541, the practice of witchcraft in England, was declared a crime punishable by death, so arrangements were put in place to hold trials of suspects and to agree the method of carrying out the sentence – usually by burning or drowning. When animals or people suddenly fell ill, when items were stolen or lost, or when violent unexplainable events took place, a link was created between these events and some unfortunate and unpopular local woman who became branded as a witch. Such a link is clearly recorded in J. Anderson's collection of *Ballads in the Cumberland dialect* in his account of *Grizzy the Witch*. Poor Grizzy is clearly blamed for all local mishaps in this catalogue of unfortunate events, whilst the description given of her appearance would be enough to frighten anyone away:

GRIZZY

The witch wife begged in our back
But crept away unsarra'd in ther pet
Oor Etty she churned an churned' But butter nivver cam
The pezstack fell an fadder got crush'd
Mi mudder cowp'd over an leamed hersell
Wee Jenny's pet lamb droon'd I'the well.
Aul Grizzy the witch as fwolk will say
Meks ointment for sair een
An cures the toothache wi a charm
O hard words wi the bible seen
She milks the kye – the urchin's bleamed
She bleets the com wi her bad eye
When crossed by lasses – thery pruive wi bairn.
When deef Dick Maudlin lost his wife
An sed ———
When Jenny's black filly kicked a foal
When heuf bin Calep fell ower the scar
When Martin Magret burnt her frock

When smuggler Mat got lost I'the snow
When wheezing Wully was bad
Aul Grizzy ay gat the weyte of it aw.
Her face is leyke the stump ov a yak
She stoops an stutters, sheks an walks
Brear eye'd an tuthless, wid a geet beard
She coffs an groanes an mumps an talks
She lives in a hill hoose, burns whins an sticks
An theer has dealings wi the deill
Oh were she soon but cowpt into her grave
For all she leaves few can do weill.

J. Anderson

1590 KING JAMES of ENGLAND and SCOTLAND

Having married Anne of Denmark in 1590, King James, a devout Christian and scholar, later responsible for producing the King James Bible, was returning with his bride from Scandinavia to Scotland, when his ship encountered *"the most terrible and violent of storms"*. It was suggested to him that dark arts were being used against him by his enemies, and upon his eventual safe return, King James immediately set up a group to investigate and advise on how to deal with the increasing menace of witchcraft. Two years later, over 60 witches, whose leader in Berwick was one Agnes Sampson, were found guilty after confessing under torture that they had acted on behalf of the devil against the King. Such findings fuelled the King's determination to take steps to convince his subjects of the threat to society and religion from witchcraft. Those steps were to establish a system of investigation, trial, torture, confession and punishment of all witches culminating in their eradication by death.

By 1597, King James had published a compendium called *Daemonology* – a treatise which served as a political and theological guide to tell ordinary people about the danger that witches posed to society.

In his introduction, King James claimed:

"The fearfull abounding at this time in this countrie, of these detestable slaves of the devil – the witches – or enchanters – hath moved me – beloved readers – to dispatch in this following treatise of mine – to resolve the doubting – both, that such assaults by Satan are most certainly practised, and that the instrument thereof merits severely to be punished."

DAEMONOLOGIE,

IN FORME OF A

DIALOGVE,

Diuided into three Bookes,

WRITTEN BY THE HIGH
AND MIGHTIE PRINCE,
IAMES by the Grace of GOD King of
England, Scotland, France and Ireland,
Defender of the Faith, &c.

THE PREFACE
to the Reader.

HE feare-full aboun-dinge at this time in this countrie, of these detest-able slaues of the Deuill, the Witches or enchaun-ters, hath moved me (beloued reader) to dispatch in post, this following treatise of mine, not in any wise (as I protest) to serue for a shew of my learning & ingine, but onely (mooued of conscience) to preasse thereby

TO THE READER.

thereby, so farre as I can, to resolue the doubting harts of many, both that such assaultes of Sathan are most certainly practized, & that the instrumentes thereof, merits most severly to be punished: against the damnable opinions of two principally in our age, wherof the one called SCOT an Englishman, is not ashamed in publike print to deny, that ther can be such a thing as Witch-craft: and so mainteines the old error of the Sadducees, in denying of spirits. The other called VVIERVS, a German Phisition, sets out a publick apologie for al these craftes-folkes, whereby, procuring for their impunitie, he plainely bewrayes himselfe to haue bene one of that profession. And for to make this treatise the more pleasaunt and facill, I haue put it in forme of a Dialogue, which I haue diuided into three bookes: The first speaking

1580 to 1640 Law Courts take over

Following the Witchcraft Act of 1542, the responsibility for charging and trialling of witches was removed from the church, and placed with the Law Courts – trials reaching their peak between 1580 and 1640 when over 500 were put to death.

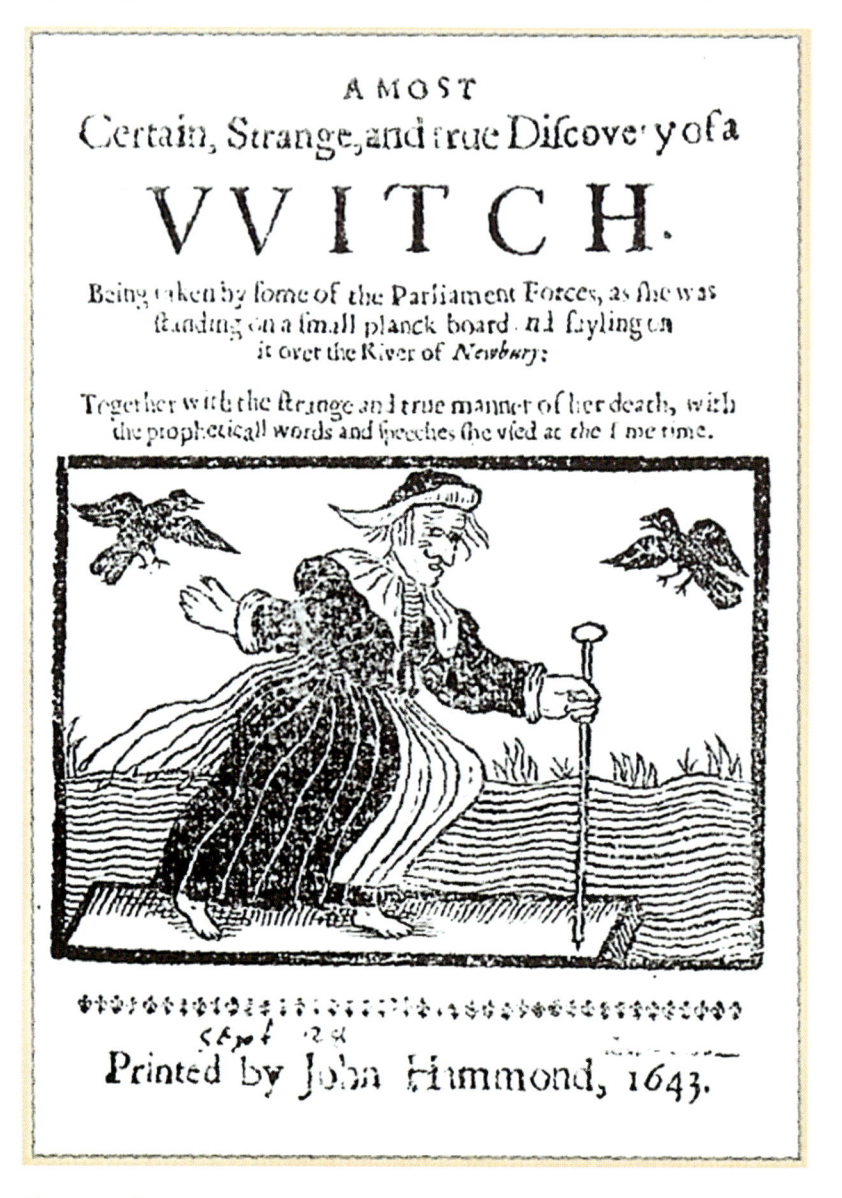

Title page of "A most certaine, strange, and true discovery of a witch" 1643

7. WITCHCRAFT OVER THE CENTURIES

In 1637 the Governing Charter of Carlisle granted by Charles 1st records the appointment of two Aldermen to act as Justices of the Peace with particular authority to:

> *"investigate all manner of felonies, poisonings, enchantments, witchcrafts, magic, art, trespasses, forestalling, regratings, engrossing and extortions."*

The Audit Books of the City of Carlisle between 1649 and 1650 reveal that the two Aldermen fulfilled these duties, for which they were generously rewarded:

Royal Charters of City of Carlisle 1649 – 1650 (above and over the page)

£6.10s seems to be a very generous salary and mirrors similar arrangements elsewhere in the country.

Item pd for takeing the waters course beyond the Cittie ditche		00:02:06

May 1650:

3 — Item pd the Clarke for writeing out the Bookes		00:05:00
Item pd for two roape to the swine heards		00:09:10
4 — Item pd for birk rodd for Cham Pearson		00:00:08
7 — Item in wine & sack upon the Shereiff witch tryer bestowed		00:04:00
Item pd to the witch tryer		06:10:00
8 — Item pd for wine & sack when Governour came from London		00:08:06
Item pd for letters to the poste Maister		00:01:06
10 — Item pd to a Blinde pwiist		00:05:00
12 — Item pd to a soger wch came out of Ireland		00:02:06
13 — Item pd an Irish man his wife & 3 children		00:05:00
14 — Item pd for 2 soldiers wch came out of Ireland		00:02:00
15 — Item pd to John Nirkholson to carrie him to his folkinde		00:07:00

Item for ye Wytch fynder

7. WITCHCRAFT OVER THE CENTURIES

Mathew Hopkins 1650

In 1650, Matthew Hopkins was appointed Witchfynder General and had 68 witches put to death in Bury St. Edmunds; 19 hanged at Chelmsford; whilst at Aldeburgh, he was paid £6 for a day's work clearing the town of witches; at King's Lynn £15; and a very grateful Stowmarket paid him £23 – all at a time when the average daily wage was 2.5p.

> *"Certain 'tests' were invented to determine whether a person was a witch or not. Mary Sutton of Bedford was put to the swimming test: with her thumbs tied to opposite big toes, she was flung into the river. If she floated then she was deemed guilty and therefore punishable by death; if she sank she was to be considered innocent – but the verdict often arrived too late for the unfortunate innocent victim to recover from the ordeal."*
>
> Matthew Hopkins, *Witch Finder*, 1650

From the *Register Of Deaths of Lamplugh* in Cumberland, from January 1658 to 1663, amongst the recorded causes of death are:

> *"Frightened to death by fairies (3)*
> *Bewitched (4)*
> *Old women drowned upon trial by witchcraft (3)."*

In Westmorland, local cattle had become ill with disease, and several farmers, instead of endeavouring to find a cure, took it into their heads that the old hag, The Witch of The Wold had brought this calamity upon them. The farmers assembled with pitchforks and staves, and surrounded the Witch's house, convinced that in addition to their ailing livestock, young Jackie's fits had come upon him the very day that he had passed close to the witch's cottage. The angry mob applied the test: they tied her legs and arms together and threw her into the river – it having been decided beforehand that if she were to swim then she was certainly a witch and would be burnt. If she were to sink, then she could be declared as innocent. So, the poor wretch had little chance of either survival or justice.

By 1672 people were becoming more educated and enlightened and were developing sufficient courage to become more sceptical about witchcraft.

By 1735 – when Lizzie Douglas was just six years old, witchcraft had ceased to be a crime in England, but many people continued to "believe" – possibly due to ignorance, reluctance to change, or, more importantly, as some measure of insurance – just to keep on the safe side – in case it might all be true! Following this change in the law, many well educated women saw this as an opportunity to prosper and earn a lucrative living by exploiting the popular beliefs and superstitions of simple people – that illness, sudden crises, astonishing events and visions of the future, all had their origins in the supernatural. And so they set themselves up as fortune tellers, soothsayers or "wise women" – and it is in this climate that Lizzie Baty may well have commenced her apprenticeship.

Changes in society in the 1800s and improving widespread education led to fading beliefs in witchcraft. Many witch stories reflect the social, religious and moral concerns of past generations, and as society had become more educated, most people now had sufficient confidence to dismiss such stories as folklore.

But, despite the changes in the law, witch hunting continued – until as recently as 1863 when a witch was drowned in a pond in Headingham. Across the 18th and 19th centuries witchcraft continued to hold a grip on the popular mind for several generations, particularly in rural areas. In 1945 a person thought to be a witch in Essex was murdered by being pinned to the earth with a pitch fork.

In 2002, Victoria Klimbie, an eight year old girl from the Ivory Coast was beaten to death by her foster parents in London, firmly believing that she was a witch. They had taken her to a church to be exorcised and claimed that she was possessed by evil spirits and the devil and the only answer was to put her to death.

And, finally *The Daily Telegraph* of October 2018 refers to an astonishing report from the Department of Education:

> **Rise in children beaten to drive out 'evil spirits'**
>
> Cases of children being beaten or abused in witchcraft rituals or to drive out evil spirits have increased sharply in the past year. Social workers recorded 1,630 cases compared with 1,460 in the previous 12 months. The figures from the Department for Education are based on child referrals to local authorities. Leethen Bartholomew, head of the National FGM Centre, said disabled children were particularly at risk within communities that believed it was a sign they were possessed.

Peter Burn, in 1864 published a booklet *Local traditions and other poems* which contains the poem *Wise Women*. This poem questions the morality of exploiting the superstitions of simple folk, preferring instead to trust to education and religion:

WISE WOMEN

Is it true what people tell us
Of the doings of these women
Great in art and great in cunning?
Is it true they boasted powers
Which by far exceeded human?
That up springing at their bidding
Came disasters to their neighbours?
Strange the doings of these women
(So the old folk love to tell us)

LIFE IN BRAMPTON WITH LIZZIE THE WITCH

All we read of in the stories
Of the witches and the fairies.
Happen'd to the simple people
In those days of superstition.
When they suffer'd loss from robbers
Off they hastened to consult them;
Nought could happen but they knew it,
Be it good or evil fortune.
They would hear their sad complainings
And would cheer them with the promise
Of their losses brought unto them;
And such promise, quick an often.
Prov'd the substance of their wishes
When we call to mind the power,
They had gain'd and held amongst them
We may cease to guess and wonder,
Why so anxiously they sought them,
In their crosses and distresses.
Tell us, ye who boast of wisdom,
What hads made thes women famous?
Were they skill'd in art, or magic?
Were their powers more than human?
That their lives were more than common?
None are bold enough to question;
That they sway'd the lives of others-
Is as true and doubly certain.
Mind is power; they possessed it,
And the foolish people felt it;
They were conscious of this power,
And they made it serve their purpose
Actuated by the knowledge
Of their being more than human,
Men and women fram'd their actions

7. WITCHCRAFT OVER THE CENTURIES

To their promptings, sayings, teachings.
More they knew than books had taught them
They had studied living volumes
They had studied human nature;
And with tact and worldly shrewdness,
Pry'd into the lives of others –
Read their longings and endeavours,
And, enabled by experience,
Guess'd and told them of the future
Gone those days of mental darkness
Men have outliv'd superstition
They have learnt to trust to nothing
But which bears the name of wisdom,
And confess no other power,
Than the God of earth and heaven

Peter Burn

Fear of, and respect for, witchcraft continued to be widespread in the 19th century in Brampton. Stories of witches and their exploits flourished as families gathered around the fireside, whilst newspaper reportage regularly fuelled superstition in an effort not only to convince, but also to entertain and shock readers. Many people retained a quiet scepticism on the one hand, whilst at the same time, being reluctant to dismiss "believing" altogether – "just in case".

Lizzie was tolerated by the folk of Brampton – those who would meet her in the street would be sure not to cross her path but preferred to keep a safe distance. Many were unsure as to whether to greet her and in doing so, risk offending her, or to ignore her completely, thereby inviting a curse to descend upon them. Some believed that by shaking hands with Lizzie, good fortune would be bestowed upon them.

Sir Walter Scott in his Border Waverley novels based many of his stories on anecdotes garnered from local people. When visiting Gilsland and proposing marriage to his beloved Mademoiselle Charpentier at the "Popping stone" he gathered many a local tale to convert into his story of Meg Merrilees and Guy

Mannering. He may well have heard directly of the activities of *"Lizzie o'Branton"*. Meg is quoted by Walter Scott as *"having dealings with the deevils"*. Lizzie's ability to reveal the secret places where stolen property had been concealed, and her readiness to help friends with her mysteriously acquired knowledge, comes pretty near to some of the revelations of Meg Merrilees in Scott's novel *Guy Mannering*.

Mother Shipton was said to be one Ursula Southiel – a wise woman who could detect a thief and could ensure the safe return of stolen property. She later became famous for predictions and was widely reported as a soothsayer who could cast spells. Later, however, the publisher Richard Head confessed that he had invented most of the stories attributed to Mother Shipton, followed by the author Charles Hindley, who admitted that he had faked much of the stories in 1873 in order to generate income from the sales of his newspapers.

Chapter 8

CONCLUSIONS

The Old English word *"witch"* meant *"one who casts a spell"* and *"witchcraft"* meant *"using magic to harm humans, farm animals, or property"*. It is almost always a woman and is generally stated or implied that her powers came from the devil. Fear of and respect for witchcraft, features within all periods of history but it was as late as the 15th century that it was generally perceived as a threat to society with laws forbidding its practice and declaring it as being punishable by death.

Mystery and superstition surround the life of Lizzie the witch so her story is incomplete. There are certain facts which can be confirmed from archives, but what about the rest? In our endeavour to separate truths from the complex mixture in the cauldron of legend and folklore there still remain some doubts lurking in the depths of our imaginations that refuse to be extinguished.

Why has belief in witchcraft survived over the centuries and still remains today in some folk? Is it a response to our fears or anxieties associated with death; the future; of sudden unexplained events; bad luck or illness? Such fears and anxieties provide a fertile ground for the germination of stories, of wild explanations and imaginings, which can become acceptable and believable in the minds of those looking for explanations or solutions to such mysteries. Is there some hidden pressure in our subconscious urging us not to dismiss such beliefs "just in case" and to protect ourselves from becoming the hapless victims of destiny?

Whether the Lizzie stories are real or imagined is perhaps irrelevant. They do exist and possibly serve to guide us through the challenges of good and evil. Perhaps they also deserve to exist as part of our fascinating legacy of folklore.

BIBLIOGRAPHICAL REFERENCES

Allsopp, J. *Nanny the Witch of Denton*
Anderson, J. *Collection of Ballads in the Cumberland Dialect*
Burn, Peter. *Local Traditions, Poems and Wise Women*, 1864
Burn, Peter. *English Border Ballads*, 1870
Burn, Peter. *Rosenthal Publ.*
Carlisle Journal, March 10th 1817
Carlisle Journal, Mary Bateman 25.3.1809 P.4
Carlisle Journal, 27/11/1896; 29/1/1896; 7/7/1933; 25/12/1953
Carlisle Patriot, 29/1/1896; 11/3/1817
Corporation of Carlisle Chamberlain's Accounts, Vol 3, 1630 – 1674
Cowper, H.S. *Cumbrian Folklore*, C.W.A.A.S., Sept 1896
City of Carlisle account book, May 1650, CRO Ca/4/3
Cumbria Record Office *The Brampton Witch*, DX/275/5
Cumberland News, 29/1/1986
Cumberland News, 10/9/1993; 10/12/2010
Diocese of Carlisle: Marriage Licence Bonds, CRO, 1740 – 1752
Ferguson, R.S. *Royal Charters of City of Carlisle*, 1894
Gibson, Thomas. *Legends and Historical notes of North Westmorland*, 1885
Hall, A. *Lakeland legends and folklore*, 1977, Jackson Collection, I.D.398.2
Hammond, John. *A most certain, strange and True Discovery of a Witch*, 1643
Head, Richard. *Mother Shipton*
Henderson, W. *Folklore of Northern Counties of England and Borders*, 1879
Holder, G. *Paranormal Cumbria*, 1A 133, Jackson Collection

BIBLIOGRAPHICAL REFERENCES

Marlow, Christopher. *Doctor Faustus*
Marriage Register Brampton Old Church, 1751
Register of Deaths in Lamplugh Cumbria Archive Office
Scott, Sir Walter. *Demonology and Witchcraft*
Scott, Sir Walter. *Guy Mannering*
Sutton, Alfred. *Witches and Witchcraft*, 1896, Carlisle Scientific Society
The Howsonian
The News, December 17th, 1896
Whitehead, Anthony. *Legends of Westmorland*, 1896
Wilkie, M.S. *Border Customs and Superstitions*, Jackson Collection
Wilson, Thomas. *The Pitman's Pay and other poems*, 1843

BY THE SAME AUTHOR

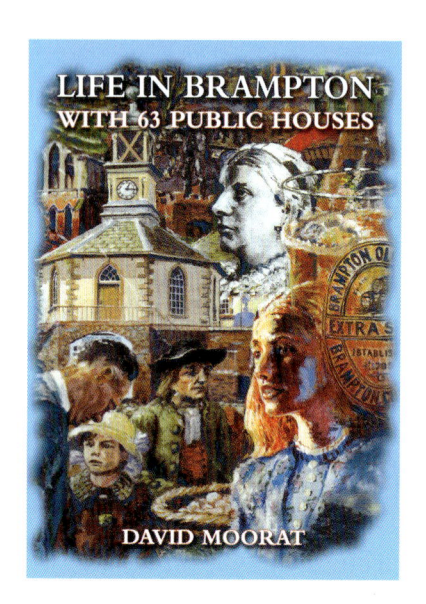

LIFE IN BRAMPTON WITH 63 PUBLIC HOUSES

David Moorat's gazetteer of the surviving pubs of Brampton is a grand read. But more than that, it shines a light into dark corners of forgotten history; into the dusty attics where the really interesting snippets of past lives linger. If like me, you tend to remember pubs as navigation aids you'd better set aside a couple of days for the journey next time you venture Brampton way.

History Into Print, 978-1-85858-313-6, £12.95

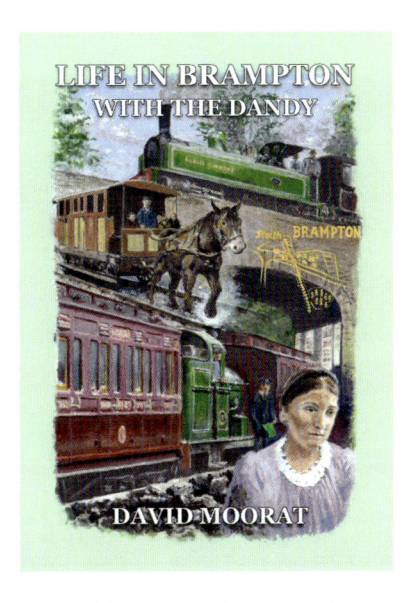

LIFE IN BRAMPTON WITH THE DANDY

Travelling arrangements for rail passengers to Brampton, have been the subject of scathing reports over the past 182 years:

"…having booked a ticket for Brampton our traveller will discover as he alights from the train that Brampton is yet a further two miles away and that he is obliged to pay for and embark upon a further stage of his journey in a Dandy wagon in which passengers are huddled together, first drawn by a horse and then run down an incline without motive power until he is landed at a coal staith. Here, he discovers that he is still three quarters of a mile from the centre of Brampton – a journey he must then complete on foot."

What were the reasons for this unfortunate state of affairs for travellers, and why was the name Dandy given to this uncomfortable mode of travel?

David Moorat's research sets out to trace the events, retells the incidents which took place and discusses the social and political pressures that brought about this frustrating set of circumstances that has left Brampton town still without a convenient railway station.

History Into Print, 978-1-85858-351-8, £8.95

Both titles are available to order now at: www.historyintoprint.com